Introducing The Old Man

St Joseph the Carpenter

A Hidden Gem In Christianity

MARIA ISKANDER

Introducing The Old Man

St Joseph The Carpenter

A Hidden Gem In Christianity

©Maria Iskander 2021

First published 2021

ISBN: 978-0-6450222-9-2

All rights reserved. Without limiting the rights under copyright reserved above, no part of this publication may be reproduced, stored in or introduced into a database and retrieval system or transmitted in any form or by any means (electronic, mechanical, photocopying, recording or otherwise) without the prior written permission of the owner of the copyright.

Acknowledgements

I would like to dedicate this book to Fr Moussa Soliman. Fr Moussa Soliman was the pioneer of the first Queensland Coptic Orthodox church- St Mary and St Joseph's Church at Coopers Plains. May his memory and legacy of love, be forevermore. Amen.

For my Confession Father - Fr Elijah Iskander.

For my brother- John Iskander.

Contents

Acknowledgements iii

Chapter One
Introducing the 'Old Man' 1

Chapter Two
Pure and Righteous Man 11

Chapter Three
Obedient of God's plan 19

Chapter Four
Faithful to God 27

Chapter Five
Wise as a Serpent, Harmless like a Dove 35

Chapter Six
A Merciful Heart 45

Chapter Seven
Good Teacher 53

Chapter Eight
A Sanctified Man 63

Chapter Nine
Golden Silence 71

Chapter Ten
Miracle Worker 77

Chapter One

Introducing the 'Old Man'

Growing up with a father who was a doctor, my family and I were always considered as a privileged, high class majority in the community. Let that sink in. With no merit of our own, taken into consideration, we received upmost respect and attention. How ridiculous you may think? Well, I could not blame you to think that way. For I too, agree. Despite this, on a personal level, I enjoyed my childhood being filled with my "Old Man's" providence of health-related stimuli and books, in place of creepy porcelain dolls.

As society and psychology attest, fathers play a vital role in providing their children with golden 'nuggets' of wisdom. Fortunately, my brother and I were not exempt of this. My brother and I- competitive by nature, in nearly everything from board games, soccer matches, to time lapses of toilet runs, were given a golden 'nugget' of wisdom that forever changed our perspectives on victory. I reminisce on how our father took us outside in the park, to then lecture us on how society often pressures people to be on the winning side than the losing side. Apart from the context of rooting for underdog soccer teams, he emphasised how underdogs are in fact, more relatable and make people happier when they are victorious. At first, my brother and I were sceptical. After all, who would willingly support and give praise for someone almost predestined to lose? So, in our father's efforts with validating an underdog's mental toughness, St Joseph the Carpenter's (St Joseph) life and legacy, was set on limelight. And as a result, my brother and I's perspective on what makes someone victorious, changed forever.

Travelling 12,204 km from Australia, St Joseph's birth location is traced. Born and brought up in the city of Bethlehem and town of Judea, St. Joseph came from royal lineage. Pure Evangelists- St Luke and St Matthew, mark this royal lineage being from the greatest king of Israel- King David (See Matthew 1:1-16 and Luke 3:23-38).

In saying that, these Holy Scriptures do not tell us why or when St. Joseph left Bethlehem for Nazareth to be his place of residence. Apart from being of royal lineage, we also know for certain that St Joseph worked as a carpenter (Matthew 13:55).

A carpenter is someone whose trade comprises of cutting, shaping and installing building materials. During the Roman Empire period (30-33AD), carpenters would provide woodwork services to help build and maintain the following: roofs, doors, ship decks, lintels, shelves, cabinets, tables and panelled rooms. However, only the wealthy could afford these woodwork services. Hence, for the peasants and poorer families, carpenters provided woodwork services that comprised of constructing ladders, wheels, yokes for the animals, and farm implements.

While some lumber might have been available locally from suppliers, most carpenters went to the woods themselves to choose the type of wood that would suit.

The work they were doing. Isaiah the prophet described this work, in the following passage:

"The carpenter stretches a line, he marks it out with a pencil; he fashions it with planes, and marks it with a compass; he shapes it ... He cuts down cedars; or he chooses a holm tree or an oak and lets it grow strong among the trees of the forest; he plants a cedar and the rain nourishes it" (Isaiah 44:13-15).

Sounds like a sophisticated profession. Are we right?

Well, one could not be blamed for immediately thinking just that. For in the ancient world's Northern America region, carpenters were deemed as highly skilled workers, who made a high income; and ranked as middle classed individuals in the social hierarchy. Nevertheless, in the anthropology of peasant societies in Jerusalem i.e. Nazareth, carpenters were ranked beneath peasant farmers. In other words, carpenters were the lowest classed individuals within the social hierarchy. Fortunately for St Joseph, God had a plan to elevate his social standing to be much more than a 'simple carpenter'.

According to tradition, when St. Mary, who was dedicated to the temple, completed twelve years in the sanctuary, she was no longer permitted to stay there any longer. As a result, the Jewish priests announced throughout all of Judea, on the requirement of a respectable man from the tribe of Judah. Defying social expectations, St. Joseph was included as a potential candidate. What is more, by God's grace, St Joseph- an 'underdog' in this selection process, was the subject of a miracle. This miracle began when the priests gathered twelve righteous men from the tribe of Judah. Following this, the priests took the men's staffs inside the sanctuary; to then discover a dove resting on the staff that belonged to St. Joseph. At this scene, the priests immediately knew that this was a sign of God's will; and the righteous St. Joseph took St. Mary to his house.

"Isn't this the son of Joseph?" (Luke 4:22)

Undeniably, St Joseph's profession was not admirable in the eyes of others. Yet, God had a plan for him. God had a plan for the carpenter to be the father of all fathers- Jesus Christ.

By taking Mary as his wife and naming the child Jesus (the name given to him in the dream), Joseph was claiming the divinely born child as his own. As Dodson said, "Joseph adopted Jesus as his son". And in a sense, as Dodson continues, through Jesus Christ coming to earth, taking on our flesh, and going through the process of birth, death to a glorious resurrection; Joseph provided the power of our adoption into the family of Christ.

Sayings of the Saints

"When your children are still small, you have to help them understand what is good. That is the deepest meaning of life".

+ Elder Paisios

"In children we have a great charge committed to us. Let us bestow great care upon them and do everything that the Evil One may not rob us of them".

+ Excerpt from St. John Chrysostom, Homilies on 1 Timothy, Homily 9

"We take all care indeed to have our farm in good order, and to commit it to faithful manager.... But we do not look out for what is much more important, for a person to whom we may commit our son as the guardian of his morals, though this is a possession much more valuable than all others. It is for him indeed

that we take such care of our estate. We take care of our possessions for our children, but of the children themselves we take no care at all. Form the soul of thy son aright, and all the rest will be added hereafter".

+ Excerpt from St. John Chrysostom, Homilies on 1 Timothy, Homily 9

"Where there is intellect, there always will be knowledge. Still, you must educate the child. Teach the boy and girl geography and history; but if you do not train the child's will, in order not only to please you, its parents, but to bend before the holy will of Him, who is the only just rewarder of good and evil, then you are a failure as a Christian. Where there is no discipline, there is no constancy".

+ St Sebastian Dabovich, "On the Education of Children," Preaching in the Orthodox Church: Lectures and Sermons by a Priest of the Holy Orthodox Church

"Love, harmony and understanding between parents are what are required for the children. This provides a great sense of security and certainty."

+St. Porphyrios

Reflection Questions

1. **What pressure/s did you experience growing up as your father's child?**

   ....
   ....
   ....
   ....
   ....
   ....

2. **Did you have any privilege/s growing up as your father's child?**

   ....
   ....
   ....
   ....
   ....
   ....

3. **What is the most important lesson you have learned from your father?**

   ....
   ....
   ....
   ....
   ....
   ....

4. **The rituals and traditions that my father brought into our family were as follows:**

   ....
   ....
   ....
   ....
   ....
   ....

5. **What was your father's hometown like?**

   ....
   ....
   ....
   ....
   ....
   ....

6 a. **Have you visited your father's hometown. Describe the best parts of it.**

   ....
   ....
   ....
   ....
   ....
   ....

Chapter One: Introducing the 'Old Man'

6 b. If you have not visited your father's hometown, do you ever intend to?

....
....
....
....
....
....

7. What did your father most like about moving to a new country? Explain

....
....
....
....
....
....

Life Challenge

Fathers wear a lot of hats. We know this. They spread their time across many roles. How do they do it all? How do they manage being a husband, father, employee/ employer, leader and/or church volunteer?

Here is my challenge to you: show active interest in your father's life.

You can achieve this challenge by doing the following:

(1) Ask your father for details about his job and day.

(2) Find out what he is up to around the house.

(3) Peruse a couple of the books/magazines he reads or the Tv shows/films he watches.

(4) Make an investment in what your father values.

These initiatives are all a great way to show respect to your 'old man's values.

Chapter Two

Pure and Righteous Man

"Do good, Lord, to those who are good, to the upright of heart" (Ps 124:4)

The Psalm above suggests that since the Lord blessed St Joseph to have God the Son and the Mother of God, in his family, he must have been "good and upright of heart".

St Joseph and St. Mary had determined to keep their betrothment sacred and pure to God. So, when St Mary was with child, St Joseph was greatly grieved by this and was considering what to do. As St Matthew wrote: Joseph was "a just man", an upright man. He was "unwilling to put [Mary] to shame" and so "resolved to send her away quietly" – a very respectable thing to do. Nevertheless, when the angel of the Lord appeared to him and told him, "that which is conceived in her is of the Holy Spirit" (Matt 1:20), he accepted this divine incarnation with no question.

On top of St Joseph vowing to take care of St Mary, he also obeyed the orders by Archangel Gabriel, for the second time. The second apparition required him to take St. Mary and the Child Jesus to Egypt for refuge. Egypt was chosen as the place of refuge because of King Herod's unrighteous anger in Bethlehem.

Archangel Gabriel appeared to St Joseph for the third and final time. After announcing that King Herod had died, St Joseph and his family were no longer bound to 'stay low and survive. And so, after staying two years living in the land of Egypt; St Joseph, St Mary, and the Child Jesus, returned to the humble city of Nazareth.

Aside from approximately five verses in the Gospels of the New Testament, little is mentioned in the Holy Bible about St Joseph. Indeed, apart from his work as a carpenter and his sharing of St Mary's anxieties, we do not really know much more about him. In fact, there is not a single word of St Joseph recorded in the Holy Bible. Readers and Christians only know him by what he did (Matt 7:16). All in all, this proves that St Joseph was not a man who was known by his knowledge of the Scriptures, but of his quietness and righteousness.

The last time that St Joseph is mentioned in the Holy Bible, is when he and St Mary found the Lord Jesus Christ- who was twelve at the time; preaching in the temple and enthralling the Jewish scholars (Luke

2:41-50). It is believed that St Joseph departed this world shortly after this event took place. According to scholars, the Lord Jesus Christ was present at his departure; and laid His hands upon St Joseph's eyes. At the time of his departure, St Joseph was one hundred and eleven years old! Moreover, his departure was in the sixteenth year of the Lord Jesus Christ.

Sayings of the Saints

"What saves and makes for good children is the life of the parents in the home. The parents need to devote themselves to the love of God. They need to become saints in their relations to their children through their mildness, patience, and love".

+St. Porphyrios

"Parents need to make a new start every day, with a fresh outlook, renewed enthusiasm, and love for their children. And the joy that will come to them, the holiness that will visit them, will shower grace on their children".

+St. Porphyrios

"With us everything should be secondary compared to our concern with children, and their upbringing in the instruction and teaching of the Lord".

+St. John Chrysostom

"The primary goal in the education of children is to teach, and to give examples of a virtuous life".

+St. John Chrysostom

"Conquer men by your gentle kindness, and make zealous men wonder at your goodness. Put the lover of justice to shame by your compassion. With the afflicted be afflicted in mind. Love all men but keep distant from all men".

+ St. Isaac the Syrian, The Ascetical Homilies of St. Isaac the Syrian, Homily 64, "On Prayer, Prostrations, Tears, Reading, Silence, and Hymnody"

"My brethren, do all that is in your power not to fall, for the strong athlete should not fall, but, if you do fall, get up again at once, and continue the contest. Even if you fall a thousand times, because of the withdrawal of God's grace, rise again at each time, and keep on doing so until the day of your death. For it is written: 'If a righteous man falls seven times,' that is, repeatedly throughout his life, 'seven times shall he rise again' [Proverbs 24:16]".

+ St. John of Karpathos, From the collection of letters to monks in India

Chapter Two: Pure and Righteous Man

Reflection Questions

1. **What is a good memory you have with your father?**

   ....
   ....
   ....
   ....
   ....
   ....

2. **How did your father make you feel special?**

   ....
   ....
   ....
   ....
   ....
   ....

3. **What did you learn about love and relationships from your father?**

   ....
   ....
   ....
   ....
   ....
   ....

4. **What brought your father great comfort and peace? Example: Fishing**

   ....
   ....
   ....
   ....
   ....
   ....

5. **What quality/qualities of your father, do you wish to maintain? Explain why**

   ....
   ....
   ....
   ....
   ....
   ....

Life Challenge

Here is my challenge to you: Write your dad a letter.

Phone calls and texts are nice. Emails are convenient. Handshakes and hugs bring warmth to the heart and soul. But to write your father a letter- there is nothing quite like it.

You can achieve this writing challenge by doing the following:

Chapter Two: Pure and Righteous Man

(1) Write down how much you appreciate your father's leadership in your life.

(2) Write down one favourite memory you have with your father- in vivid detail.

(3) Name two to five things you love most about your father.

Chapter Three

Obedient of God's plan

There is something about our fallen nature that compels us to be disobedient. Take it from someone who is stubborn, sometimes my disobedience would be blatant and full-blown in fact. Fortunately, for most of the time, our disobedient tendencies can be more subtle like when our mother encouraging us to eat our fruit and vegetables, or to read a book. We have been all guilty of it.

According to the Catechism (2199): *"This commandment of obedience includes and presupposes the duties of parents, instructors, teachers, leaders, magistrates, those who govern, all who exercise authority over others or over a community of persons".*

Out of the many wonderful attributes of St Joseph, obedience is one worth highlighting. As written in the Holy Bible; St Joseph was obedient to God's will, throughout his entire life.

To start off, St Joseph was obedient to heeding God's will, when Archangel Gabriel announced the virginal birth of the Messiah; and that St Mary would be his wife (Matthew 1:20-24). With no pride, St Joseph accepted this instruction; thereby fulfilling the prophet Isaiah: *"Therefore the Lord himself shall give you a sign: the maiden is with child and she will bear a son, and will call his name Immanuel"* (Isaiah 7:14). This can make us reflect on how often our pride can unknowingly get in the way of God's great plans for us.

The second instance of St Joseph's obedience was when he led his family for refuge in Egypt. As Matthew 2:13 says:

"Now when they had departed, behold, an angel of the Lord appeared to Joseph in a dream and said, 'Rise, take the child and his mother, and flee to Egypt, and remain there until I tell you, for Herod is about to search for the child, to destroy him'".

Let us delve deep into what St Joseph was facing in this moment: a death threat. King Herod the infidel king of Bethlehem, wanted to kill our Lord Jesus Christ: The Messiah of the world, and the son of God! As most of us have heard of the biblical story; we can too often overlook the severity of the situation. However, St Joseph did not. Combined with St Joseph being a carpenter by trade, Egypt being six hundred and ninety-two kilometres away- being a thirty-day travel by foot, and not knowing the Egyptian language, St Joseph followed through. He accepted

Chapter Three: Obedient of God's plan

to travel to a land that he never had been to before. A land where his ancestors were persecuted for two hundred and fifteen years. Hence, we could not blame him if Egypt was not the first place he would consider going for refuge. Nonetheless, St Joseph just went. And, without further ado,

Egypt became the Holy Family's country of refuge; from King Herod's infanticide in Bethlehem (Matthew 2:13-15).

Two years later, St Joseph displayed another act of obedience, when Archangel Gabriel commands him and the Holy Family to leave Egypt. St Joseph did not have a timeline in his life. He lived in the present and thereby was capable of obeying God's will at every time.

Thus, he showed no hesitation to Archangel Gabriel's commands; and led the Holy Family to settle in a modest city: Nazareth (Matthew 2:19-20). St Joseph's obedience in this final instance, also fulfilled which was spoken by the prophets on our Lord Jesus Christ: "He shall be called a Nazarene" (Matthew 2:23).

St Joseph was a true man of obedience. He did exactly what the Lord asked of him, every time, and without delay. He lived the fourth commandment to the letter. Therefore, he is a model of obedience that we should all aspire to follow more diligently.

Sayings of the Saints

"Be zealous of the fulfillment of His will on earth, as it is in heaven. Forgive them that trespass against you with joy, as a good son rejoices when he has a chance of fulfilling the will of his beloved father".

+ St. John of Kronstadt, My Life in Christ.

"The grace of the Holy Spirit which is given mystically to every Christian when he is baptized acts and is manifested in proportion to our obedience to the commandments of the Lord. That is, if a Christian obeys the commandments of the Lord more, grace acts with him more, while if he obeys them less, grace acts within him less".

+ St. Nikodemos of the Holy Mountain, Christian Morality.

"The gateway to divine repentance has been opened: let us enter eagerly, purified in our bodies and observing abstinence from food and passions, as obedient servants of Christ who has called the world into the heavenly Kingdom. Let us offer to the King of all a tenth part of the whole year, that we may look with love upon His Resurrection".

+Sessional hymn, Matins, Cheesefare Monday.

"One should not oppose authorities who act for good, so as not to sin before God and be subjected to His just chastisement: Therefore whoever resists

the authority resists the ordinance of God, and those who resist will bring judgment on themselves (Romans 13:2)".

+ St. Seraphim of Sarov, "The Spiritual Instructions to Laymen and Monks", printed in Little Russian Philokalia: St. Seraphim of Sarov.

"The truly intelligent man pursues one sole objective: to obey and conform to the God of all. With this single aim in view, he disciplines his soul, and whatever he may encounter in the course of his life, he gives thanks to God for the compass and depth of His providential ordering of all things".

+St. Anthony the Great, The Philokalia.

"How will it be with us in the future life, when everything that has gratified us in this world: riches, honors, food and drink, dress, beautifully furnished dwellings, and all attractive objects—how will it be, I say, when all these things leave us—when they will all seem to us a dream, and when works of faith and virtue, of abstinence, purity, meekness, humility, mercy, patience, obedience, and others will be required of us?".

+St. John of Kronstadt.

Reflection Questions

1. **Has God ever directed you to do something that seemed impossible? What was it?**

   ....
   ....
   ....
   ....
   ....
   ....

2. **Is God directing you to do something now that appears too big or too outlandish? What is it?**

   ....
   ....
   ....
   ....
   ....
   ....

3. **In what areas in your life do you redefine your obedience to God?**

   ....
   ....
   ....
   ....
   ....
   ....

Chapter Three: Obedient of God's plan

4. In what areas of your life do you have the most difficulty obeying God?

....
....
....
....
....
....

5. In what way do you believe that living a completely obedient life can cost you your career, friendships, and social status?

....
....
....
....
....

6. In what areas are you using your hard work, sacrifice, or generosity to make up for being disobedient?

....
....
....
....
....
....

7. What are you doing today that reflects your will and not God's will?

....
....
....
....
....
....

Life Challenge

Here is my challenge to you: Reflect on St Joseph's life of obedience.

(1) Imagine yourself in St Joseph's place in the events mentioned above.

(2) Think about your own life and where you have been called to obedience.

(3) Think about your own life and where you are now being called to obedience. Pick something you have been ignoring, delaying, or flat out rejecting; and just do it. Do it for yourself. Do it for St Joseph. You will find yourself surprised by the blessings that come from your obedience.

Note: Remember that obedience extends beyond just our parents.

Chapter Four

Faithful to God

"You have been faithful over a little, I will set you over much; enter into the joy of your Master" (Matthew 25:23).

The end of the famous Parable of the Talents connects the joy of the Lord to the following virtue: Faithfulness. Moreover, this parable highlights the importance of being faithful over the little things; to relay the same faithfulness for the big things. To put it in other words, faithfulness leads from what is smallest up to what is greatest, from the care of what is entrusted to us on this earth, right up to eternal glory. Faithfulness is a virtue that must be renewed throughout one's life.

For example, married people renew their love every day—especially on anniversaries—and thus they purify it and make it grow constantly. Apart from the marriage context, faithfulness is a journey that requires us to renew our decisions in every facet of life.

Biblical scriptures place further emphasis on unconditional aspect of faithfulness; and how every person is called to respond to God's faithfulness. The Covenant with God, Christ's faithfulness, are the foundations and models of human fidelity.

Perhaps the most significant foundations of St Joseph and St Mary's model character, was their unconditional faithfulness to God.

In accordance, Johnston writes: *"God picked [St Joseph] and St Mary for this solemn responsibility in parenting Jesus, and they both accepted the challenge. For St Joseph, it is a big leap of faith, but in the example of other saints, he believes and says 'Yes' to God".*

In the limited knowledge we have about St Joseph, we see a man who only thought of serving St Mary and our Lord Jesus Christ- never himself. At the same time, what many may see as sacrifices on St Joseph's part; were in fact, acts of faithfulness.

Besides, none of St Joseph's words are even written in the Holy Bible. However, we can clearly see that by his actions, he was a just, loving, and faithful man. This confirmation dissipates the common misconception on Christianity's influence being solely based on preaching with words alone. For, as St James the apostle wrote in his book, the genuineness of the Christian's faith, can be only confirmed by actions- not just words (James 2:17). Generally, every recorded decision and act of faith made by the great St Joseph; is the golden standard for men and fathers to follow today.

God has a plan for every person, even if the one concerned does not know it. God will reward each person's faithfulness to their vocation. St Joseph's vocation was carpentry. He was a simple carpenter who served his neighbours through his handiwork. He taught our Lord Jesus Christ on the value of hard work. He led as a man of faith when he obeyed God in all things. He led as the family provider by working long hours in his carpentry workshop; to make sure the Holy Family had enough to eat and a roof over their heads. Finally, he led as a teacher by teaching Jesus his trade and how to live and work as a man.

Clearly, we can all learn a great lesson from St Joseph's faithfulness. He, who is also the patron saint of workers, is a prime example for us to value our daily vocation. And thereby use our vocation to glorify God, support our families and contribute to greater society.

Sayings of the Saints

"You need not be despondent. Let those be despondent who do not believe in God. For them sorrow is burdensome, of course, because besides earthly enjoyment they have nothing. But believers must

not be despondent, for through sorrows they receive the right of sonship, without which is impossible to enter the Kingdom of Heaven".

+ St. Barsanuphius of Optina, quoted from Living Without Hypocrisy: Spiritual Counsels of the Holy Elders of Optina.

"Do not reckon as a truly wise man that one whose mind is subject to fear on account of temporal life."

+ St. Isaac the Syrian, "Six Treatises on the Behaviour of Excellence", Mystical Treatises by Isaac of Nineveh.

"The truly intelligent man pursues one sole objective: to obey and to conform to the God of all…. For knowledge of God and faith in Him is the salvation and perfection of the soul."

+ St. Anthony the Great, "On the Character of Men and on the Virtuous Life: One Hundred and Seventy Texts," Text 2, The Philokalia: The Complete Text (Vol. 1).

"We have very little faith in the Lord, very little trust. If we trusted the Lord as much as we trust a friend when we ask him to do something for us, neither we as individuals nor our whole country would suffer so much."

+ Elder Thaddeus of Vitovnica, Our Thoughts Determine Our Lives: The Life and Teachings of Elder Thaddeus of Vitovnica.

"God 'tested Abraham' (cf. Gen. 22:1-14), that is, God afflicted him for his own benefit, not in order to learn what kind of man Abraham was – for He knew him, since He knows all things before they come into existence – but in order to provide him with opportunities for showing perfect faith".

+ St. Mark the Ascetic, "On the Spiritual Law: Two Hundred Texts" No. 203, The Philokalia: The Complete Text (Vol. 1).

"You should be afraid not of cholera, but of serious sins, for the scythe of death mows a person down like grass even without cholera. Therefore, place all your hope in the Lord God, without Whose will even the birds do not die, much less a person".

+ St. Anthony of Optina, Living Without Hypocrisy: Spiritual Counsels of the Holy Elders of Optina.

"To have faith in Christ means more than simply despising the delights of this life. It means we should bear all our daily trials that may bring us sorrow, distress, or unhappiness, and bear them patiently for as long as God wishes and until He comes to visit us. For it is said, 'I waited on the Lord and He came to me".

+ St. Symeon the New Theologian.

Reflection Questions

1. **Describe your faith in God right now**

   ....
   ....
   ....
   ....
   ....
   ....

2. **How are our difficulties linked up to our opportunities to grow in faith?**

   ....
   ....
   ....
   ....
   ....
   ....

3. **What aspect of God's faithfulness is commonly forgotten?**

   ....
   ....
   ....
   ....
   ....
   ....

4. **Where is God's greatest symbol of faithfulness seen?**

   ....
   ....
   ....
   ....
   ....
   ....

5. **How many Biblical verses state, "the just shall live by faith"? What are they and how are they used?**

   ....
   ....
   ....
   ....
   ....
   ....

Life Challenge

Here is my challenge to you: Meditate on God.

(1) Reflect on what God has done for you this year. This includes how He has s ministered His love to you, and how He has allowed you to minister His love to others.

(2) If you regularly journal (or want to begin), record on God's faithfulness in your life.

(3) Vocalise Biblical verses that promote faith.

These Biblical verses include, but are not limited to, the following:

"Do not be anxious about anything, but in every situation, by prayer and petition, with thanksgiving, present your requests to God" (Philippians 4:6).

"I can do all things through Christ who strengthens me" (Philippians 4:13).

"Whoever believes in me, as Scripture has said, rivers of living water will flow from within them" (John 7:38).

"Therefore, I tell you, whatever you ask for in prayer, believe that you have received it, and it will be yours" (Mark 11:24).

"And without faith it is impossible to please God, because anyone who comes to him must believe that he exists and that he rewards those who earnestly seek him" (Hebrews 11:6).

If you are not regularly meditating on God's Word, then it is not affecting you like it should. Remember time is no excuse. It can be done in less than five minutes. The important part is your heart. Humble your heart as you start. Do not resist the teaching of the passage because of your sin.

Chapter Five

Wise as a Serpent, Harmless like a Dove

"Behold, I send you out as sheep amid wolves. Therefore, be wise as serpents and harmless as doves" (Matthew 10:16).

When you think about high-risk jobs, what comes to mind? Bull riders, Competitive eaters, stuntmen, race car drivers, bungee jumpers, test pilots and soldiers? One would not judge you for thinking about these jobs alone. However, what if I told you that being a Christian is a high-risk job? Would you believe it? Jesus did.

Too often as Christians, we can feel the tension between feeling like we are being taking advantage of; and feeling like we are taking advantage of other people. Hence, this is where the Biblical simile: "Wisdom like a serpent and gentleness like a dove" (Matthew 10:16), come into play.

So, what does it really mean to be wise as a serpent gentle as a dove? And what does it have to do with overcoming spiritual warfare?

To consider the latter question, spiritual warfare is an active aggression from the enemy. This aggression is meant to intimidate us; thereby keeping us away from realizing God's plan for our life and business. It is the daily struggle we face as Christians as we attempt to obey the Lord Jesus Christ and His commandments.

In Matthew 10:16, Jesus announced to His disciples: *"Behold, I send you out as sheep in the midst of wolves..."* This was not just true for the early disciples. This is just as true, if not more so, for all of us in this current day. From public life at church, services, school, work, the shopping centres; to the private life in our homes, we go through struggles and operate among wolves.

Why the wolf's metaphor, you may ask?

To begin with, wolves are aggressive predators. Each day, they intentionally try to bring harm to their prey- primarily sheep. Sheep are weak and vulnerable. So, without a Shepherd on site, sheep cannot survive a wolf's attack.

Like sheep, we must carefully obey the instructions of our Shepherd- our Lord Jesus Christ; and stay close to Him to survive.

Therefore *"Be wise as serpents and harmless as doves"*, is a metaphor coined by our Lord Jesus Christ on how to not only survive, but on how to live. He takes two animals whose characteristics are complete opposite and instructs us to imitate them. One of the animals he instructs us to mirror- serpent, is the very beast that the Devil used to cause Adam and Eve to sin against God in the Garden of Eden. While the other animal- dove, is the sacrificial animal, which was typically used in worship before God during the Old Testament period. To summarise, the Holy Bible typically presented snakes as the symbol of evil power and chaos, while a dove was typically presented as a symbol of purity and innocence. Such opposites of character, represents what we as Christians, need to manifest to overcome the daily predatory aggression of the enemy- the Devil.

Drawing back to St Joseph, one cannot deny that he was the epitome of someone 'Wise as a serpent and harmless like a dove'. St Joseph seamlessly manifested this blended personality trait. He used it to protect the Holy Family from the works of the devil; thereby forwarding our Lord Jesus Christ's agenda on this Earth.

St Joseph was wise to understand people and situations. For instance, he was wise to keep St Mary's divine pregnancy a secret; before being reassured by Archangel Gabriel that St Mary would be divinely protected. Likewise, he demonstrated keen and unusual discernment when dealing with the Bethlehemites on the place for St Mary to give birth. Sure, the place ended up being an unassuming manger.

Nevertheless, St Joseph's discernment to accept the manger, fulfilled the prophecies of the Lord's birth in a manger (Micah 4:8).

Apart from discernment, St Joseph had the ability to be shrewd. Shrewd means to be practical. Indeed, St Joseph was shrewd in leading the Holy family to Egypt for refuge. He was shrewd in adapting to the Egyptian culture and lifestyle. As a result, St Joseph succeeded in protecting, and financially supporting the Holy Family through his vocation: carpentry.

To be harmless like a dove, is to lack the capacity to injure or to be free from inflicting physical or mental damage. Other Biblical translations use "innocent" or "inoffensive" instead of "harmless" for this verse. According to the Oxford dictionary, to be innocent is to be harmless in effect and/or intention.

Doves are not referred to as the birds of 'peace' for no good reason. Unlike the intimidating magpies, a dove's temperament is calm, and their disposition is sweet. Doves do not bite or swoop at humans. At most, doves might slap you with a wing if they are guarding the nest; or do not want to be picked up. All in all, doves really are harmless.

About St Joseph, there is no denying he was a gentle man. He, like Father Abraham, was able to realize the assignment that God the Father gave Him. St Joseph translated a harmless nature that was capable to protect our Lord Jesus Christ for sixteen years; and thereby expand the Kingdom of God more than any of his contemporaries.

Sayings of the Saints

"You cannot be too gentle, too kind. Shun even to appear harsh in your treatment of each other. Joy, radiant joy, streams from the face of one who gives and kindles joy in the heart of one who receives. All condemnation is from the devil. Never condemn each other, not even those whom you catch committing an evil deed….. Keep away from the spilling of speech. Instead of condemning others, strive to reach inner peace. Keep silent, refrain from judgement. This will raise you above the deadly arrows of slander, insult, outrage, and will shield your glowing hearts against the evil that creeps around".

+ St. Seraphim of Sarov.

"Do not reckon as a truly wise man that one whose mind is subject to fear on account of temporal life".

+ St. Isaac the Syrian, "Six Treatises on the Behaviour of Excellence", Mystical Treatises by Isaac of Nineveh.

"Let everything take second place to our care of our children, our bringing them up to the discipline and instruction of the Lord. If from the beginning we teach them to love true wisdom, they will have great wealth and glory than riches can provide. If a child learns a trade, or is highly educated for a

lucrative profession, all this is nothing compared to the art of detachment from riches; if you want to make your child rich, teach him this. Don't think that only monks need to learn the Bible; Children about to go our into the world stand in greater need of Scriptural knowledge."

+ St. John Chrysostom, Homilies on Ephesians, Homily 21.

"A man who is wrathful with us is a sick man; we must apply a plaster to his heart – love; we must treat him kindly, speak to him gently, lovingly. And if there is not deeply-rooted malice against us within him, but only a temporary fit of anger, you will see how his heart, or his malice, will melt away through your kindness and love – how good will conquer evil. A Christian must always be kind, gracious, and wise to conquer evil by good".

+St. John of Kronstadt, "My Life in Christ".

"The sensible man remembers all his sins from childhood onwards; he remembers them with the fear of God and with the expectation of suffering for his sins; and so, when suffering does fall on him, through either his friends or his enemies, from men or from evil spirits, either sooner or later, he at once knows the causes of his suffering, for he knows and remembers his sins".

+ St. Nikolai Velimirovich.

Reflection Questions

1. List and describe three ways you can be wise as a serpent

....
....
....
....
....

....
....
....
....
....

....
....
....
....
....

2. List and describe three ways you can be harmless like a dove

....
....
....
....
....
....

....
....
....
....
....

3. Who can you be gentler with? Explain why.

....
....
....
....
....
....

3b. What contexts should you be gentler in? Example: At church/ At home. Explain.

....
....
....
....
....

4a. Who should you be wise with ? Explain why.

....
....
....
....
....

4b. What contexts should you be wise in? Example: At work/school. Explain.

....
....
....
....
....

The **"Three R"** model: **R**elate, **R**espect and **R**esist.

Here is my challenge to you: Follow through the **"Three R"** model.

1. **Relate:** Invest time to befriend and build relationships with people where you live, work, study, and/or play. When we invest time to befriend and build a relationship, we learn about people. Learning about people entails discovery of their interests, triumphs, trials, and other circumstances. Wisdom helps us to realize the importance of relationships. Furthermore, wisdom helps us to admit that sometimes when we are preoccupied with our work, school, families and church services, we forget to invest in our relationships. Hence, wisdom helps us to reassess our priorities and time management; to make changes in our lives; and thereby maintain holy relationships.

2. **Respect:** Respect all people as God's image bearers. As Christians we must show respect to others by embodying purity, innocence, and simplicity. Like Jesus Christ's disciples and seventy- two apostles, we too must desire to see everyone come to faith in Christ. Like these pioneers of the Christian faith, we must display a humble spirit, pure intentions, and upmost respect; to gently touch people with God's love.

3. **Resist:** Resist the rant. Ranting on social media platforms, or any other platform, is not wise or harmless. Help people discover the reality of the transforming life of Christ. Help people see the value of abundant eternal life that is available every day. It is wise to publicly display a life that transcends this material world. Likewise, it is harmless to **promote Jesus Christ**, rather than just your awesome local church and its amazing people.

Chapter Six

A Merciful Heart

"Blessed are the merciful: they shall have mercy shown them" (Matthew 5:7).

The Bible verse above highlights one Beatitude. A Beatitude can be described as a sharing in the Divine Life; all of which ultimately leads to our eternal happiness with God. It is always a joyful experience for us to read and reflect on the Beatitudes! Jesus proclaimed them in his first great sermon, preached on the shore of the sea of Galilee. There was an exceptionally large crowd, so Jesus went up on the mountain to teach his disciples. That is why the Gospel is largely known as *"The Sermon on the Mount"*. Further, in the whole Gospel (Luke 1:68-79), Jesus Christ made promises for blessing according to an individual's actions. In the end, we can agree that being blessed is a desirable gift for everyone. As St. John Chrysostom expands: *"To be blessed is so great a good, that bad men and good men wish for it"*.

All in all, these Beatitudes offer us a way of life that promises eternity in the Kingdom of Heaven. At the same time, these Beatitudes provide peace; particularly during the inevitable trials and tribulations that we all face, on this earth. As the Catechism eloquently put it: *"The Beatitudes purify our hearts to teach us to love God above all things".*

"Oh, give thanks to the Lord, for He is good! For His mercy endures forever.... To Him who alone does great wonders; To Him who by wisdom made the heavens; To Him who laid out the earth above the waters; To Him who made great lights; The sun to rule by day; The moon and stars to rule by night, For His mercy endures forever" (Psalm 136:1-9).

When we give mercy to one another, we allow the experience of mercy from a magnanimous God- a God who loves us out of total gratuitousness. No one can buy God's mercy from their own merit. Mercy, like salvation, is solely given from God's loving-kindness to all of us.

For St Joseph, God showed mercy towards him in many ways. First, when he was chosen by a divine sign, to be betrothed to the Virgin and Theotokos- St Mary. This divine choosing of Fatherhood to the Messiah, elevated St Joseph from being underestimated as only a carpenter. In addition, God showed mercy to St Joseph by keeping his covenant with him. Hence, St Joseph, despite old age, was shown mercy from

Chapter Six: A Merciful Heart

God; and have survived for the first sixteen years of Jesus Christ's life on earth.

According to Jesus Christ, "Mercy is what pleases God, not sacrifice" *(Matthew 9:13; 12:7)*. St Joseph pleased God by showing mercy to everyone and every place he went. Indeed, this humble carpenter by trade, showed and received mercy; all of which ignited his energy and purpose on this earth. Like St Joseph, we must adhere to do the same.

Now as all of us in this technological age, work in different human professions, have our own homes, belong to many different countries and have different languages; we all have a greater expectation to extend God's mercies to others. For instance, somebody hurt you so bad, and they are totally in the wrong. You just cannot let it go. You cannot be in the same room as them. And the idea of doing a nice deed for them, is out of the question. But Jesus Christ says: "I am giving you other ways to give and do mercy; and as I have died for your sins, I want you to give mercy to others when they do not deserve it too".

Now, while deeds are the best way to show mercy to someone, Jesus Christ also asks us to show mercy through our words. We can do this by uttering kind words and prayers for others. However, for people who are not the kindest, even saying kind words, can be hard. Nevertheless, we can simply not wish ill of anyone. After all, if St Joseph did not wish ill of the unkind Pharisees who put down his status as a 'carpenter'; who are we to not show mercy to unkind people?

James 2:13 says: *"You must show mercy to others, or God won't show mercy to you . . . But the person who shows mercy can stand without fear at the judgment".*

This Bible verse says that the person who shows mercy, can stand without fear on the judgement day. So, if we want to be in Jesus Christ's Kingdom like St Joseph, the following is required of us: To do what is right with others, to love being merciful to others, and to live humbly in fellowship with God.

Sayings of the Saints

"You are to show mercy to your neighbors always and everywhere. You must not shrink from this or try to excuse or absolve yourself from it. I am giving you three ways of exercising mercy toward your neighbor: the first- by deed, the second – by word, the third – by prayer. In these three degrees is contained the fullness of mercy, and it is an unquestionable proof of love for Me. By this means a soul glorifies and pays reverence to My mercy" (Diary Entry, Year 742)

+St Faustina

Chapter Six: A Merciful Heart

"According to thy mercy, pour out upon me, who am miserable, at least one small drop of grace to make me understand and be converted, that I might make at least some small effort to correct myself. For if thy grace does not illumine my soul, I will not be able to see the carelessness and negligence that the passions have produced in me through my apathy and recklessness".

+St Ephraim the Syrian, 69: The Wiles of the Enemy and the Resources of Sin," A Spiritual Psalter or Reflections on God.

"The drunkard, the fornicator, the proud—he will receive God's mercy. But he who does not want to forgive, to excuse, to justify consciously, intentionally ... that person closes himself to eternal life before God, and even more so in the present life. He is turned away and not heard [by God]".

+Elder Sampson, Orthodox Word #177, "Discussions & Teachings of Elder Sampson".

"When you are about to pray to our Lady the Holy Virgin, be firmly assured, before praying, that you will not depart from her without having received mercy. To think thus and to have confidence in her is meet and right. She is, the All-Merciful Mother of the All-Merciful God, the Word, and her mercies, incalculably great and innumerable, have been declared from all ages by all Christian Churches;

she is, indeed, an abyss of mercies and bounties, as is said of Her in the canon of Odigitry".

+ St. John of Kronstadt, My Life in Christ.

Reflection Questions

1. What does it mean to be merciful?

....
....
....
....
....

2. How has God showed mercy in your life?

....
....
....
....
....

3. What does mercy reveal about God's character?

....
....
....
....
....

4. Describe one example of God's mercy in the Holy Bible

....
....
....
....
....

Important Note:

If we measure out harsh judgment, refuse to forgive, and show no mercy to those seeking it, this is how God will measure it back to us when we stand before Him. Likewise, if we measure out compassion and understanding instead of harsh judgment- showing great mercy; then this is how God will deal with us.

Life Challenge

Here is my challenge to you: Feed the Hungry, Give Drink to the Thirsty; and Clothe the Naked.

Feed the Hungry

(1) Get a group friends to help make sack lunches at your local homeless shelter.

(2) Have a food kit in your car of some non-perishable foods- in preparation for any person who may need it.

(3) Offer to pay for your friends' lunch or drink.

(4) Start a fundraiser at school to raise money for your local food shelter.

Give Drink to the Thirsty

(1) Pass out water bottles for homeless on streets with a note attached with a bible verse or a simple "you're loved."

(2) Lead a bible study with your friends and afterwards all go out for coffee.

(3) Help pass out ice cold water bottles and/or hot beverages. This could be providing water to your work colleague or making tea/coffee for a loved one at home.

Clothe the Naked

(1) Donate old or unused clothes to Goodwill, a thrift store, or a homeless shelter.

(2) Start a jacket drive at your local parish or with youth group.

(3) Send donated clothes to a missionary overseas.

(4) Pray to St. Martin and ask him to help live your live up in this clothing service to Christ.

Chapter Seven

Good Teacher

A good teacher is warm, accessible, enthusiastic, and caring to every student they teach. Hence, every student is left with a positive impact. St Joseph was a good teacher because of his approachable nature. He submitted himself to serve both the Jewish and Gentile people. Like good teachers, St Joseph employed good listening skills, and managed time for anyone who needed him.

"Then Joseph her husband, being a just man, and not wanting to make her a public example, was minded to put her away secretly" (Matthew 1:19).

To give context, after marrying Mary, St Joseph found that she was already pregnant. Thus, being a "just man", he was unwilling to put her to shame. So, like a good teacher, St Joseph perceived that shame is not an effective teaching strategy on behaviour. Hence, he showed St Mary care and compassion. As a result, Archangel Gabriel blessed St Joseph for not being invasive to St Mary; and thereby reassured him of the pregnancy being Divine- of the Holy Spirit.

"And he rose and took the child and his mother by night and departed to Egypt". (Matthew 2:14).

The Bible verse above, indicates how St Joseph had clear objectives and followed them through. Therefore, in this situation, the objective was to protect St Mary and the Child Jesus from King Herod's infanticide. St Joseph achieved this objective successfully, by leading the Holy Family to find refuge in Egypt.

In the four Holy Gospels, St Joseph was described as a "tekton," which traditionally has meant "carpenter".

At the same time, St Joseph was recorded having an incredibly positive reputation as a teacher of carpentry- in both Nazareth and Galilee. Nevertheless, we can only assume that St Joseph also taught the carpentry craft to Jesus Christ.

Sayings of the Saints

"Men are often called intelligent wrongly. Intelligent men are not those who are erudite in the sayings and books of the wise men of old, but those who have an intelligent soul and can discriminate between good and evil. They avoid what is sinful and harms the soul; and with deep gratitude to God they resolutely adhere by dint of practice to what is good and benefits the soul. These men alone should truly be called intelligent."

+ St. Anthony the Great, "On the Character of Men and

on the Virtuous Life: One Hundred and Seventy Texts," Text 1, The Philokalia: The Complete Text (Vol. 1).

"The person who loves God values knowledge of God more than anything created by God and pursues such knowledge ardently and ceaselessly".

+ St. Maximos the Confessor, Four Hundred Texts on Love 1.4, The Philokalia: The Complete Text (Vol. 2).

"The Church, through the temple and Divine service, acts upon the entire man, educates him wholly; acts upon his sight, hearing, smelling, feeling, taste, imagination, mind, and will, by the splendour of the icons and of the whole temple, by the ringing of bells, by the singing of the choir, by the fragrance of the incense, the kissing of the Gospel, of the cross and the holy icons, by the prosphoras, the singing, and sweet sound of the readings of the Scriptures."Book St John Kronstadt My Life in Christ".

+ St. John of Kronstadt, My Life in Christ.

"My child, just read! The Holy Spirit Who, through inspired men, wrote these divine words, will hear, will understand and will hasten to your assistance; and the demons will understand will sense and will flee from you. That is: He Whom you invoke for assistance will understand, and those whom you wish to drive away from yourself will understand. And both goals will be achieved".

+ St. Nikolai Velimirovich, Prologue of Ochrid.

"If you wish, the Lives of the Saints are a sort of Orthodox Encyclopedia. In them can be found everything which is necessary for the soul which hungers and thirsts for eternal righteousness and eternal truth in this life, and which hungers and thirsts for Divine immortality and eternal life. If faith is what you need, there you will find it in abundance: and you will feed your soul with food which will never make it hungry".

+ St. Justin Popovich, Orthodox Faith & Life in Christ, "Introduction to the Lives of the Saints".

"In order to fulfill the commandments of Christ, you must know them! Read the Holy Gospel, penetrate its spirit and make it the rule of your life".

+ St. Nikon of Optina.

"We think we know a lot, but what we know is very little. Even all those who have striven all their life to bring progress to mankind — learned scientists and highly educated people — all realize in the end that all their knowledge is but a grain of sand on the seashore".

+ Elder Thaddeus of Vitovnica, Our Thoughts Determine Our Lives.

"We spare neither labors nor means in order to teach our children secular sciences, so that they can serve well the earthly authorities. Only the knowledge of the holy Faith, the service of the Heavenly King are a matter of indifference to us. We allow them to attend spectacles but we care little whether they go to Church and stand

within it reverently. We demand an account from them of what they learned in their secular institutes—why do we not demand an account from them of what they heard in the Lord's house?".

+ St. John Chrysostom, Twenty-first Homily on the Epistle to the Ephesians.

"Let us ask what the goal of education is, if it is not the enlightening of man, the illumining of all his abysses and pits, the banishing of all darkness from him. How can man disperse the cosmic darkness that assails him from all sides, and how can he banish the darkness from his being without that one light, without God, without Christ? Even with all the light that is his, man without God is but a firefly in the endless darkness of this universe".

+ St. Justin Popovich.

"We may study as much as we will but we shall still not come to know the Lord unless we live according to His commandments, for the Lord is not made known through learning but by the Holy Spirit.

+St. Silouan the Athonite.

"Brethren and fathers, God, who fashioned us and brought us out of non-existence into being, has placed us in this life as in a schoolroom to learn to gospel of his kingdom."

+St. Theodore the Studite.

Reflection Questions

1. **What are the qualities of a good Christian teacher and mentor?**

   ....
   ....
   ....
   ....
   ....
   ...

2. **What was the best word of advice you have heard from your Christian teacher/ mentor?**

   ....
   ....
   ....
   ....
   ....

3. **What have your Christian teacher/ mentor taught you, on how to keep a meaningful relationship with God?**

   ....
   ....
   ....
   ....
   ....

   ....
   ....

Chapter Seven: Good Teacher

....
....

4. How do you respond to constructive criticism?

....
....
....
....

5. In what area, is God leading you, to improve your life?

....
....
....
....
....

6. Describe your preferred teaching style at Mainstream school? Explain why.

....
....
....
....
....

7. Describe your preferred teaching style at Sunday school? Explain why.

....
....
....

Life Challenge

Some of our best teachers in life, are not immediately present with us today. Hebrews 12 begins with the words, *"Therefore, since we are surrounded by so great a cloud of witnesses . . ."* This phrase follows a long listing of biblical people who were examples of good teachers and faith.

Here is my challenge to you: Write up a list and surround yourself of people who are good teachers in your life.

(1) Write a list: people who are important in your local congregation, pastors/priests who guided you, parents who taught you the faith, Sunday school teachers and/or mentors who helped you grow.

(2) Gather with other teachers and small group leaders to share your stories and questions about how God has called you.

Questions to use for sharing:

- What do you think God wants of each of you?
- What gifts do you see in yourself?
- How does your experiences with God help teach and model prevenient grace?
- What gifts do you see in others, and that inspire you?

Chapter Seven: Good Teacher

- Why are respectful and healthy relationships important in the Sunday school teaching ministry?

- What hesitancies or self-doubts do you still carry? Explain why.

- How might you work together in different ways to enhance the Sunday school teaching ministry?

Chapter Eight

A Sanctified Man

Sanctification. According to the Oxford dictionary, sanctification is the action of making or declaring something holy. Moreover, in Hebrew, the word sanctification means qadash. Like the Oxford dictionary definition, the Hebrew word means "people or things holy and set apart". In this turbulent time we live in, God is looking for godly men and women set apart from evil ways and actions. God is looking for sanctified individuals, filled with the power of the Holy Spirit, and anointed for the glory of God and His service.

It is a pious belief that St. Joseph was sanctified before his birth. Such a concept is not original. In fact, this concept was preached at the Council of Constance; and recorded in the Gospel of St Luke. To focus on the latter, the Gospel of St Luke, detailed the process of pre-sanctification on the beloved cousin of Jesus Christ-St John the Baptist.

Regarding the writings of the Church Fathers, no one can doubt that St Joseph was a sanctified man. Indeed, St Joseph's elite level of sanctification, made him deemed worthy by God; to guard, provide, protect and be the head of the Holy Family. Being a sanctified, mature man, St Joseph completely surrendered to the work of God in his life.

St. Joseph was never carried away by any unsound doctrines. He was deeply rooted in the Word of God. Moreover, he did not live to please men; or live in secret sin. Rather, St Joseph loved to share his faith; and realisation that God chose him and St Mary to fulfil the prophecies on the Messiah's birth. Indeed, St Joseph along with St Mary, both lived their lives to glorify God- and God alone.

Overall, St Joseph's sanctified nature, makes him a role model for chastity and purity- especially for husbands, fathers, and young men.

Sayings of the Saints

"Our religion is perfectly and profoundly conceived. What is simple is also what is most precious. Accordingly, in your spiritual life engage in your daily contest simply, easily, and without force. The soul is sanctified and purified through the study of the Fathers, through the memorization of the psalms and of portions of Scripture, through the signing of hymns and through the repetition of the Jesus Prayer.

Chapter Eight : A Sanctified Man

Devote your efforts, therefore, to these spiritual things and ignore all the other things".

+St. Porphyrios.

"Children, I beseech you to correct your hearts and thoughts, so that you may be pleasing to God. Let us therefore strive to preserve the holiness of our souls and to guard the purity of our bodies with all fervor. Ye are the temple of God, says the divine Apostle Paul; If any man defile the temple of God, him shall God destroy."

+ St. Nicholas of Myra, The Great Collection of the Lives of the Saints.

"It should be known, however, that the unclean spirits obey human beings in two ways. Either they are rendered submissive to the holiness of the faithful through divine grace and power or, having been soothed by sacrifices and by certain songs of the impious, they fawn over them as over friends".

+ St. John Cassian.

"People with families are also called to holiness, as are those in all kinds of professions, who live in the world, since the commandment about perfection and holiness is given not only to monks, but to all people".

+ Hieromartyr Onuphry Gagaluk.

Reflection Questions

1. Describe ONE person in your life who you consider as sanctified (holy) Explain why.

   ....
   ....
   ....
   ....
   ....

2. Discuss ONE saint who you admire for living a sanctified (holy) life

   ....
   ....
   ....
   ....
   ....
   ....

3. How do you define sin?

   ....
   ....
   ....
   ....
   ....

4. What makes you a strong believer in your faith?

   ....
   ....
   ....

5. Why is it important to obey God's commandments, if Christ died on the cross?

　　..
　　..
　　..
　　..
　　..

6. How are you intentional about putting away everything that is displeasing to God and living a holy life?

　　..
　　..
　　..
　　..
　　..

Life Challenge

Our Fallen state has no appetite for sanctification. So, we should not be discouraged if we are not sufficiently concerned about sanctification in our life or the lives of those around us—right now. We must remember that God gives grace to the humble. Likewise, we must remember that God is the one who does the work of making us more like Christ. Further, we participate in that work, by struggling against sin, and demonstrating a firm faith in Christ.

Here is my challenge to you: Pursue and Grow in Sanctification

(1) Reflect and repent to God on your sins.

(2) Confess your own sin—not someone else's. It is not beneficial for you to confess sins that are not yours. To make the confession process easier, you can list your sins on a piece of paper; and then recite it to your confession father.

(3) Read the Holy Bible. As written in John 15:3, when we read the Holy Bible, we become 'spiritually cleansed', inside out.

(4) Study the Holy Bible. You can do this by attending Bible studies at your local church or researching online. Studying the Holy Bible helps us better comprehend and articulate who God is, what he has done for us, and how he calls us to live-in sanctification.

(5) Pray. Praying is the first form of communication with God. It expresses our faith- and sometimes lack of faith, in the sovereign power of God. Prayer helps us to stay grounded in the messiness of this life.

(6) Find fellowship. Fellowship with others, encourages us to put our faith into practice; by loving and bearing with one another.

(7) Give to others. Giving weans our hearts off putting our trust in the fleeting things of this world i.e. money, possessions etc.

Chapter Nine

Golden Silence

"*Silence is a source of great strength"* – Lao Tzu

In this pathologically noisy world, silence is considered as equal to being alone and lonely. So, almost everyone you see walking down the street is listening to music or talking with someone. The radio and CD player is almost always turned on during car rides. Young people seem to need to have loud music playing in their ears, nearly all the time; and as a result, become incapable of being in silence for even one minute.

Now, while some people dislike a silent environment, others look forward to it. Besides giving our ears a break, and a golden opportunity to just spend time with our thoughts, silence has been shown to offer significant health advantages. From a physiological standpoint, silence helps lower blood pressure and blood cortisol levels, boost the body's immune system, and promote good hormone regulation. Turning to a spiritual perspective, silence can help one become aware of their essence, flow of life and potential.

Nevertheless, in the book: *The Power of Silence*, Cardinal Robert Sarah, affirms that silence is an essential condition for prayer- an indispensable for Christian life. The essence of the book concludes that there can be no Christian life without prayer; and there can be no prayer without silence.

St Joseph was a silent figure of the three persons in the Holy Family, but his faith spoke volumes. It is because of what he did, not what he said, that makes him a holy man. His silence allowed him to listen and respond to the calling of God. From how he looked after and served the Holy Family in Egypt, Nazareth, and Galilee; St Joseph's golden silence proves that he, after Jesus himself, is the greatest man to imitate in our daily lives. Saint Joseph was silent, but his faith spoke volumes.

Sayings of the Saints

"The Lord remained silent before Pilate and Herod; He made no attempt to justify Himself. You must imitate His holy and wise silence when you see that your enemies accuse you, with every intention of certain conviction; they accuse only with the purpose of hiding their own evil intention under the guise of judgement".

+ St. Ignatius Brianchaninov, The Cup of Christ.

Chapter Nine: Golden Silence

"Prayer is food for the soul. Do not starve the soul, it is better to let the body go hungry. Do not judge anyone, forgive everyone. Consider yourself worse than everyone in the world and you will be saved. As much as possible, be more quiet".

+ St. Joseph of Optina: Living Without Hypocrisy: Spiritual Counsels of the Holy Elders of Optina.

"The Lord shows us that we ought not to answer those who ask a question with malicious intent (cf. Mt. 21:23-27). For He Himself did not reply to those Jews who questioned Him with cunning, although He was not at a loss for an answer".

+St. Theophylact, Explanation of the Gospel of St. Matthew.

"The first stage of this tranquility consists in silencing the lips when the heart is excited. The second, in silencing the mind when the soul is still excited. The goal is a perfect peacefulness even in the middle of the raging storm".

+ St. John Climacus, Step 8.4, Ladder of Divine Ascent.

"Let us always guard our tongue; not that it should always be silent, but that it should speak at the proper time."

+ St. John Chrysostom.

"A man may seem to be silent, but if his heart is condemning others, he is babbling ceaselessly. But

there may be another who talks from morning till night and yet he is truly silent, that is, he says nothing that is not profitable".

+St. Abba Pimen.

Reflection Questions

1. Have you experienced a situation when there was deadly silence? Describe it.

   ....
   ....
   ....
   ....
   ....

2. What do you think of the moment of silence to remember the dead?

   ....
   ....
   ....
   ....
   ....

3. What do you think of governments who try to silence people?

   ....
   ....
   ....
   ....
   ....

4. What makes some people afraid of silence? Explain.

....
....
....
....
....

5. What makes some people afraid of silence? Explain.

....
....
....
....
....

Life Challenge

It is hard to find a pious person who is always talking. On the contrary, one who possesses a spirit of prayer, is a lover of silence. Since the earliest times, silence has been considered the shield of innocence, the buckler against temptations, and the fruitful source of recollection. Nevertheless, for us to practise the virtue of silence correctly; we must learn to balance when to speak, and when to be silent. As written in Ecclesiastes 3:7: *"There is a time to be silent, and a time to speak"*.

Here is my challenge to you: Entertain the silence.

(1) Walk outside. You can walk solo to get more in tune with nature. This will also allow your mind to take a quiet time-out. If walking solo is a bit daunting to start with, invite a friend. Then, make sure to walk at least part of the way, in mutual silence.

Wait in bed. Remain in bed an extra five minutes before getting up for the day. Use this time to slowly awaken to the world. Say a silent prayer of gratitude for all that you have; and ask for blessings for the day ahead.

(2) Engage. Engage in deep breathing exercises. These exercises can promote calmness and quiet at the same time.

(3) Meditate. This practice can be whatever you want it to be. From simple to more intricate meditation techniques. Teach yourself or join a class- whatever works for you. Meditation is a good habit to practise every day.

Chapter Ten

Miracle Worker

According to Merriam Webster's Dictionary, a miracle is defined as the following: "An extraordinary event taken as a sign of the power of God".

As a rule of thumb, the miracles of the Bible era, occurred in the presence of a multitude of credible witnesses—even hostile observers. For instance, when the Lord multiplied the loaves and fishes, over ten thousand people were present (John 6:10). Truly, the signs validating Christianity were never committed "undercover" (Acts 26:26).

The Christian church's records of miracles confirm the divine nature of God. Moreover, the miracles are powerful and uplifting reminders that God is still at work- in these modern, marvellous, and messy times. The miracles recorded of St Joseph in the Christian church, further elicit his great esteem in heaven, and his apt remembrance on this Earth.

Miracle one:

In the year 1852, by order of the bishop of Santa Fe, Jean Baptiste Lamy, the Chapel of Our Lady of Light was built. It was placed under the care of the Sisters of Loretto.

When the chapel was ready, builders were faced with an unexpected problem: there was no way to climb from the nave to the choir.

Despite the nuns' persistence on building a staircase, the builders told them it would be impossible. Instead of giving up, the nuns decided to pray a novena to St. Joseph- the patron saint of carpenters. After finishing the novena, a stranger appeared at the door of the chapel. The stranger was a mysterious man, and he carried a saw, a square and a few other simple tools. He looked like a professional carpenter. The nuns found it ludicrous that they had never heard or contacted him before. After agreeing to the man's conditions i.e. total privacy, the nuns allocated the man to a private chapel.

This man and stranger locked himself in the chapel for three months. What is stranger, during those three months of work, no nun or even the Mother Superior, could catch him entering or leaving the chapel. As soon as the work was finished, the man disappeared- without ever having asked for any payment for his services. As the carpenter left before the Mother Superior could pay him, the Sisters of Loretto offered a reward of money. Thus, this reward would be given to anyone who could make the identity of the carpenter known. Alas, no one ever showed up.

Being six meters high, the staircase constructed by this man, took two full turns over its axis. It was built without any nails, glue, or central support. Hence, the construction of the staircase itself, is miraculous. Moreover, architects observed that the staircase should have collapsed at the very first moment someone used

it. It was not until the year 1887, that this unusual staircase was attached to a wall. When the railing was added, the outer spiral was attached to a nearby pillar.

Since then, the miraculous carpentry of the staircase at the Chapel of Loretto (Santa Fe, New Mexico) has been attributed to St. Joseph the carpenter himself!

Miracle two:

On the Feast of the Annunciation, St. Gertrude the Great (1256-1302) had a vision. In this vision, St Mary revealed to her the glory of St Joseph. Rapt in ecstasy, she beheld Heaven open and there she saw St Joseph seated on his throne. Every time his name was pronounced, the saints reverently bent their heads in deep respect. This made St Gertrude grow in a greater love and respect for him. As a result, St Gertrude became encouraged to make intercessions in his name- especially during times of difficulties.

St. Gertrude wrote the following reflection on her miraculous vision:

"I saw Heaven opened and St. Joseph sitting upon a magnificent throne. I felt myself wonderfully affected when, each time his name was mentioned, all the Saints made a profound inclination toward him, showing by the serenity and sweetness of their looks that they rejoiced with him on account of his exalted dignity."

Miracle three:

Renowned for her good influence on her husband, and devout piety, St Margaret of Cortona (1247-1297) experienced many miracles from St Joseph's account. Hence, every day she gave homage to St Joseph. Nevertheless, on the day of her departure from the Earth, the Lord Jesus Christ appeared to her. From telling how pleased He was from her daily homage to St Joseph; St Margaret was strengthened to pass over happily and peacefully.

Prayers to St Joseph

Prayer 1

Context: According to Christian historians, this prayer was found in the 50th year of Our Lord and Saviour

Jesus Christ. Moreover, in the year 1505, the prayer was sent from the Pope Julius II, to Emperor Charles, while he was going into battle with France.

Note: Dedicate this prayer for anything you desire; and then recite it for nine consecutive mornings.

"O St. Joseph, whose protection is so great, so strong, so prompt before the throne of God, I place in you all my interests and desires. O St. Joseph, do assist me by your powerful intercession and obtain for me all spiritual blessings through your divine Son, Our Lord and Saviour Jesus, so that, having engaged here below you heavenly power, I may offer my thanksgiving and homage".

Prayer 2

Context: According to the Synaxarion, whoever reads this prayer, shall never die a sudden death, be drowned; nor shall poison take effect on them or the hands of the enemy in battle. To put it simply, whoever recites this prayer, will die a "happy and peaceful" death.

"O St. Joseph, I never weary contemplating you and Jesus asleep in your arms. I dare not approach while He reposes near your heart. Press Him in my name and kiss His fine head for me and ask Him to return the kiss when I draw my dying breath. St. Joseph, patron of departing souls, pray for me".

Life Challenge

According to the Oxford dictionary, the word "promise" means: "A covenant or declaration that one will do exactly what they say, or something will happen just as pledged". From the book of Genesis to the book of Revelations, we read of ordinary people with extraordinary faith; all of which, received the promises sealed for them, from God.

For us Christians today, these promises are sealed for us, as much as they were for our forefathers. To ponder on one promise out of the myriads recorded, Jesus Christ promised us the following:

"If you have faith as small as a mustard seed, you can say to this mountain, 'move from here to there' and it will move" (Matthew 17:20).

To put it simply, Jesus Christ promised us that miracles happen when we believe in God. And just as the Bible verse denotes, our faith can move mountains.

Here is my challenge to you: Reignite your faith in God.

(1) **Pray for the desire.**

> **Note:** To be candid, sometimes we do not want to spend time with God. From the stresses, busyness and demands from school, work, family, and friends, sometimes prayer and reading the Holy Bible, is the last thing we want to do.
>
> Over time, when you pray for the desire, you will

notice your lukewarmness transforming into an enthusiastic passion for Him.

(2) **Realise you are missing out.**

Note: It is a hard pill to swallow. But in truth, when we are not spending time with God, we miss out. There is so much encouragement, healing, guidance, blessings, faith, and other breakthroughs that we can retrieve from being in His presence.

Refer to the following Biblical references:

Encouragement*- Jeremiah 29:11; Psalms 119:11; 1 Thessalonians 5:11; Isaiah 40:31.*

Guidance*- Psalms 119:105; John 16:13; James 1:5; Psalm 32:8.*

Blessings*- John 15:1-5; Matt 6:33; Galatians 5:22-24; Isaiah 26:3.*

Faith*- Romans 10:17; Hebrews 11:1; John 8:24; Psalm 46:10.*

(3) **Find what works best for you.**

There is not a "one size fits all" approach to our lifelong journey with God. Find your love language with God.

Love languages with God

If your love language is in *meditative practises*, keep a prayer journal, attend Bible studies, and read books/devotionals.

If your love language it is in _acts of service_, donate and serve in charities and/or community projects.

If your love language is in _quality time_, regularly attend youth gatherings/worship sessions, go to coffee shop runs with spiritual mentors and listen to a sermon.

Summary

In a culture that barrels at breakneck speed on neutralising the magnitude of what it means to be a man and a woman, ample research confirms the distinctive advantages that fathers bring to children's lives. Indeed, fathers are the "underdogs" in parenting. For they, equal to mothers, are vital role models for children's upbringing and development. Drawing from a Christian perspective, St Joseph the Carpenter is an example of an "underdog" in the parenthood of Jesus Christ.

The gifts and characteristics that St Joseph the Carpenter brought to the Holy Family, are inseparable from his masculinity. All these gifts and characteristics are designated into chapters. These very chapters also inspire one to visualise and reflect on the Fatherhood of St Joseph, alongside the GOAT fathers of every reader on this Earth.

Utterly, St Joseph's confidence in his divine calling as a Carpenter, a Servant of the mystery of the Divine Incarnation, and a Father to Jesus Christ;

gives further reason for his honour and cherishment from Apostolic times.

May the blessings and prayers of St Joseph the Carpenter- the perfect example of fatherhood, be with us all. Amen.

Chapter Ten : Miracle Worker

Introducing the Old Man - St Joseph the Carpenter

www.ingramcontent.com/pod-product-compliance
Lightning Source LLC
Chambersburg PA
CBHW071353160426
42811CB00094B/284